ABC Book of Bible People

Bible Stories for Young Readers Series

Book Three

By Martha Fisher
Artist: Peter Balholm

Copyright 2004
Rod and Staff Publishers, Inc.
P.O. Box 3, Hwy. 172
Crockett, Kentucky 41413
Telephone (606) 522-4348

Printed in U.S.A.

ISBN 978-07399-2331-3
Catalog no. 2717

"Blessed is he that readeth" (Revelation 1:3).

Introduction

This series has been planned to provide good, worthwhile reading material on a level that young children can read and understand. We have endeavored to put Bible facts in simple, childlike language so that young readers can read it themselves. It is our prayer that through reading these Bible facts at an early age, the child will develop a strong faith in God, a proper fear of God, and a wealth of Bible knowledge.

We have made an effort to keep all the Bible facts Scripturally accurate. Each book is designed to teach God's overruling power, His holiness, His great love, and His watchful care over His children.

Book Three, *ABC Book of Bible People*, is a book following the alphabet. Each letter of the alphabet has several names of Bible characters and a short story about them. A Bible reference is given with each story to show where it can be found in the Bible.

The purpose of this series is to make the Bible interesting for children. When children read the Bible because of interest stirred by reading these stories, our efforts will have been well rewarded.

The theme of this series is "Blessed is he that readeth" (Revelation 1:3).

To my

nieces and nephews

Contents

Introduction 2

A—Abraham, Adam, Aaron, Abigail 6

B—Baruch, Balaam, Belshazzar, Bartimaeus 9

C—Caleb, Cushi, Cleopas, Cornelius 12

D—Dorcas, Deborah, Daniel, Demetrius 15

E—Eve, Elijah, Ezra, Eutychus 18

F—Felix, Festus, Fortunatus 21

G—Gehazi, Gideon, Goliath, Gamaliel 23

H—Hur, Hannah, Hezekiah, Haman 26

I—Isaac, Ishmael, Ichabod, Ittai 29

J—James and John, Jacob, Jeremiah, Jairus 33

K—Korah, Keturah, Kish 36

L—Lazarus, Levi, Lydia, Luke 38

M—Miriam, Mahlon, Mephibosheth, Mary 40

N—Nicodemus, Noah, Naboth, Nehemiah 43

O—Obadiah, Og, Obed, Onesimus 46

P—Peter, Pilate, Philip, Priscilla 49

Q—Quartus, Queen of Sheba 52

R—Rahab, Reuben, Rehoboam, Rhoda 54

S—Saul, Shadrach, Simeon, Stephen 58

T—Terah, Tobiah, Thomas, Timothy 61

U—Urbane, Uzza, Uzziah .64

V—Vashti 67

W—We 68

X—Xerxes 69

Y—You 70

Z—Zacchaeus, Zipporah, Ziba, Zacharias 71

Questions and Answers 75

Aa

<u>A</u>braham built an **<u>a</u>ltar** to worship God.

Abraham

Genesis 12:1–9

Abraham loved God. He believed and obeyed God. God talked to Abraham. He said, "I do not want you to serve idols as your father does. I want you to go far away from your father's house.

"Go to a land that I will show you. I will be with you and bless you. You will have many children. I will give a good land to your children." Abraham believed God. He obeyed God. Abraham made an altar and worshiped God.

Adam

Genesis 1

Adam was the very first man to live on the earth. Before God made Adam, He had made a very beautiful world. He made the trees and flowers. He made the birds and animals. God made the sun shine to give light on the earth. It was a lovely place.

But there was no one to care for the plants and animals. So God said, "Let us make man in our image." God made a man from the dust of the ground. He breathed into the man, and the man became a living soul. This was Adam, the first man. God told Adam to take care of the animals and the beautiful world He had made.

Aaron

Exodus 28, 32

Aaron was Moses' brother. God used Aaron to help Moses lead the children of Israel to the land of Canaan.

God chose Aaron to be a priest. That means Aaron talked to God for the people. When the people sinned, Aaron offered sacrifices for himself and the people. He confessed their sins to God.

One day Aaron did a very wicked thing. The people said to Aaron, "Make us gods." Aaron did what the people wanted. He made a golden calf for them to worship. God did not want His people to worship other gods. He punished Aaron and the people for doing this.

Abigail

1 Samuel 25

Abigail was Nabal's wife. She was a good and kind woman. Nabal was a selfish man. He was not kind to others.

David and his men were tired and hungry. They came to Nabal and asked him to give them some food. But he would not give them any.

Someone told Abigail what her husband had done. She was sorry her husband had been selfish. She took bread, meat, dried corn, raisins, and fig cakes, and loaded them onto donkeys. Then she hurried to David to give him all these good things to eat.

Bb

Baruch helped Jeremiah write a **book**.

Baruch

Jeremiah 36

Baruch was Jeremiah's helper. God said to Jeremiah, "The children of Israel are worshiping idols. I will punish them for this sin. Write my words in a book and read them to the people. Maybe they will repent and stop sinning."

Jeremiah told the words of God to Baruch. Baruch wrote them in a book. This book was a scroll. As Baruch wrote, he rolled the book up on one side. Then Baruch read God's words to the people.

The king heard about the book. He also wanted to hear what was in the book. He did not like Jeremiah. He did not like the book. He did not like God's Word. He did not want to obey God.

The king was sitting by the fireplace. When he heard God's words read from the book, he took his knife and cut off a piece. He threw it into the fire. Soon he cut off another and another. Finally the whole book was burned.

But this did not change God's Word. Baruch wrote God's words in a book again. God let some enemies come. They put the king in prison just as the book said they would.

Balaam

Numbers 22

Balaam was a prophet. But he was not a good prophet. He did not obey God. A king was afraid of the children of Israel. This king sent men to Balaam. They said, "Come, Balaam. The king wants you. He wants you to curse the children of Israel. Curse them and make evil things happen to them. If you do this, the king will give you a lot of money."

Balaam knew that God did not want him to curse His people. But he wanted the money. He got on his donkey and went with the men. God sent an angel to stop him. Balaam did not see the angel. His donkey saw the angel. It stopped. Three times the donkey stopped. Balaam did not know why the donkey would not go on. He hit the donkey.

Then God made the donkey do a very strange thing. It talked to Balaam. Then Balaam saw the angel. He was afraid because he knew he was disobeying God.

Belshazzar

Daniel 5

Belshazzar was a wicked king. He used the gold cups from God's temple to serve wine. The people ate and drank. They were merry. They praised the idols they had made.

Suddenly they saw fingers writing on the wall. That looked very strange. Now the king was not merry. He was very much afraid. He was so afraid that his knees shook. The king called for Daniel to tell him what this writing meant.

Daniel said, "O King, you do not obey God. God sent this hand to write on the wall. The writing says your kingdom will be taken away. You will not be king anymore."

That very night some enemies came. They killed Belshazzar and took over the kingdom.

Bartimaeus

Mark 10:46–52

Bartimaeus was blind. He could not see the pretty flowers and trees. He could not see the people. He could not see anything. Day after day he sat by the road near the city. Many people passed that way. Some people gave him money.

One day blind Bartimaeus heard the sound of many footsteps. He asked, "Why are so many people walking?"

Someone answered, "Jesus is coming this way!"

Bartimaeus called, "Jesus, have mercy on me." Someone told him to be quiet. But he called more loudly, "Jesus, have mercy on me!"

Jesus saw poor, blind Bartimaeus. He stopped. He healed his eyes. Now Bartimaeus could see. How happy he was!

Cc

Caleb went to spy out the land of **Canaan**.

Caleb

Numbers 13, 14

Caleb said, "Let us go into the good land of Canaan. God will help us!"

The children of Israel were near the land that God had promised to give them. Moses had sent twelve men to look at the land. All the men said, "It is a good land." But some of them were afraid. They said, "The people are big and strong. We cannot go into the good land."

Caleb and Joshua said, "Do not be afraid. God is with us. Let us go."

Many of the people were afraid to go. They cried that night. They did not trust God. Because they did not trust God, God did not let them go into the Promised Land.

Caleb trusted God, so he got to go into the Promised Land.

Cushi

2 Samuel 18

Cushi went with Joab and his men. They were going to fight against David's enemies. As they left, David said, "Be kind to my son Absalom." Even though Absalom was one of David's enemies, David still loved him.

David's men fought. Absalom's men fought. But David's men won. Absalom and many of his men were killed.

Joab called Cushi. "Run," he said. "Go and tell David what you saw."

Cushi ran. He found David waiting by the city gates. He told David, "Your enemies are dead."

David asked, "Is Absalom safe?"

When David knew that Absalom was dead, he cried. David said, "O my son Absalom, I wish I could have died for you."

Cleopas

Luke 24:13–35

Cleopas and his friend walked slowly home. They were talking sadly about Jesus.

Someone came near to them. He said, "Why are you so sad?"

Cleopas and his friend said, "Don't you know what happened?" ↗

"What?" He asked.

They said, "We thought Jesus was the Son of God. Then the rulers killed Jesus. Now some women told us that He is alive again!"

They did not know that it was Jesus who was walking with them. He said, "Why are you so slow to believe? The Bible says that Jesus will give His life. Then He will rise from the dead."

When they reached home, they said to Jesus, "Come in and eat with us."

They sat down to eat. Jesus took bread and blessed it. He gave them some bread. Then they knew it was Jesus who was talking to them. Now they believed that He was alive. They were very happy.

Cornelius

Acts 10

Cornelius served God. He wanted to know more about God. One day an angel talked to him. The angel said, "God heard your prayers. Now send men to call for Peter. He will tell you about God." As soon as the angel was gone, Cornelius sent three men to get Peter.

Four days later Peter came to Cornelius's house. Cornelius had asked his family and friends to come to his house and hear about God. Many people were there. Peter told them that Jesus died to save people from their sins. He said, "Whoever believes in Jesus will be saved."

Cornelius believed in Jesus. He and many of his friends were baptized.

Dd

Dorcas made **d**resses for poor people.

Dorcas

Acts 9:36–42

Dorcas was busy sewing. In and out, in and out, went her needle. Day after day she made clothes for the poor people. Everyone loved Dorcas.

One day Dorcas became sick. Now she could not sew. Soon she died. Many people gathered at her house. How sad they were! When Peter came, he saw many people crying. Some mothers were showing the clothes that Dorcas had made for them and their children.

Peter told everyone to go out of the room. He kneeled down and prayed to God. He asked God to help. Then he looked at Dorcas lying there with her eyes closed. He said, "Dorcas, get up."

Dorcas opened her eyes and sat up. God heard and answered Peter's prayer. He made Dorcas alive again!

Peter called all the people to come into the room. How happy they were when they saw Dorcas.

Deborah

Judges 4

Deborah lived in a time when many of the children of Israel were worshiping idols. Now they were in trouble. God let their enemies rule over them. This was a hard time for Israel.

After twenty years, Israel prayed to God. They asked God to help them.

God heard their prayers. He spoke to Deborah, who was a godly woman. He showed Deborah what He wanted Israel to do. Deborah called a man named Barak. She said to him, "God wants you to go and fight against the enemies. He will help you."

Barak said, "If you will go along, I will go. If you will not go, I will not go either."

Deborah said, "I will go." They obeyed the Lord and went out to fight against their enemies. The Lord helped them to win the fight. At last Israel was free from their enemies.

Daniel

Daniel 6

Daniel was living in a strange land. He was far away from home. He did not forget God. Every day Daniel prayed to God.

The king in this land liked Daniel. He liked him because he was good and obedient. So the king made Daniel his highest ruler.

Some men did not like Daniel. They wanted to be the highest rulers. They wanted to get rid of Daniel. They worked out a wicked plan and got the king to put Daniel into the den of lions.

The king was sorry. He did not want Daniel to be hurt by the lions. That night the king could not sleep. Early in the morning he went out to the lions' den. He called, "Oh, Daniel, was your God able to save you?"

Daniel answered, "God sent His angel and closed the lions' mouths."

God took care of Daniel because Daniel prayed and trusted in Him.

Demetrius

Acts 19:21–41

Demetrius was a silversmith. He made little silver models of a temple to sell. That temple was not a good temple. There were idols in that temple, and the people worshiped them. People bought the little silver temples because they worshiped the idols. Demetrius got a lot of money by selling silver temples.

Paul came to this city. He preached about Jesus. He said, "Idols that are made with men's hands are not gods."

Some people believed Paul. They believed on Jesus. They stopped worshiping idols. They stopped buying the little silver temples that Demetrius made.

Demetrius did not like this. It made him very angry. If the people believed on Jesus, they would not buy his temples.

Demetrius was so angry that he tried to hurt Paul. But God kept Paul safe.

Ee

Eve lived in the Garden of **Eden**.

Eve

Genesis 2:18–23

Eve was the very first woman. God had made Adam first from the dust of the earth. He had given Adam the beautiful Garden of Eden for his home. But Adam was lonely.

God said, "It is not good for man to be alone." So God made Adam sleep. While Adam slept, God took one of his ribs. From this rib, God made a woman. He gave the woman to Adam to be his wife. Adam called his wife's name Eve. Adam loved Eve. They were very happy in the Garden of Eden.

Elijah

1 Kings 17:1–6

Elijah was a prophet of the Lord. God sent Elijah to talk to King Ahab. Ahab was a wicked king. He did not like God's message. He did not like Elijah. He hated him so much that he wanted to kill him.

God came to Elijah again. He said, "Go and hide by the brook. You can drink water from the brook. I will send ravens to feed you."

Elijah obeyed God. He hid by the brook. The cool water in the brook was good to drink. Every day the ravens came. They flew closer and closer. They brought bread and meat for him. Down, down they came, right to Elijah. They brought bread and meat from God every day.

Ezra

Ezra 7, 8

Ezra was a scribe who wrote God's words in a book. Many Jews had gone to Jerusalem. They had built the temple of God. Ezra wanted to go to Jerusalem too. He wanted to teach the people all of God's laws.

The king said Ezra could go to Jerusalem. He said all the Jews who wanted to go to Jerusalem could go. Ezra would teach them God's laws.

Ezra met with the Jews who wanted to go to Jerusalem. They knew it was a long, long way to Jerusalem. They knew they would go through many dangerous places. But they knew God would take care of them.

Eutychus

Acts 20:7–12

Eutychus climbed the steps. Up, up, up he climbed to the third floor. He wanted to hear Paul preach. The room must have been full of people. Eutychus sat in an open window. He listened. Paul kept preaching. It was getting late. It was past midnight. Eutychus was so sleepy. His head began to nod, and soon he fell fast asleep.

Suddenly Eutychus fell out of the window, down to the ground. His friends ran down the stairs and outside. Eutychus lay quiet and still. He was dead. Paul went down. He put his arms around him. He said to the people, "Do not be afraid. His life is in him." How happy they were! Eutychus was alive!

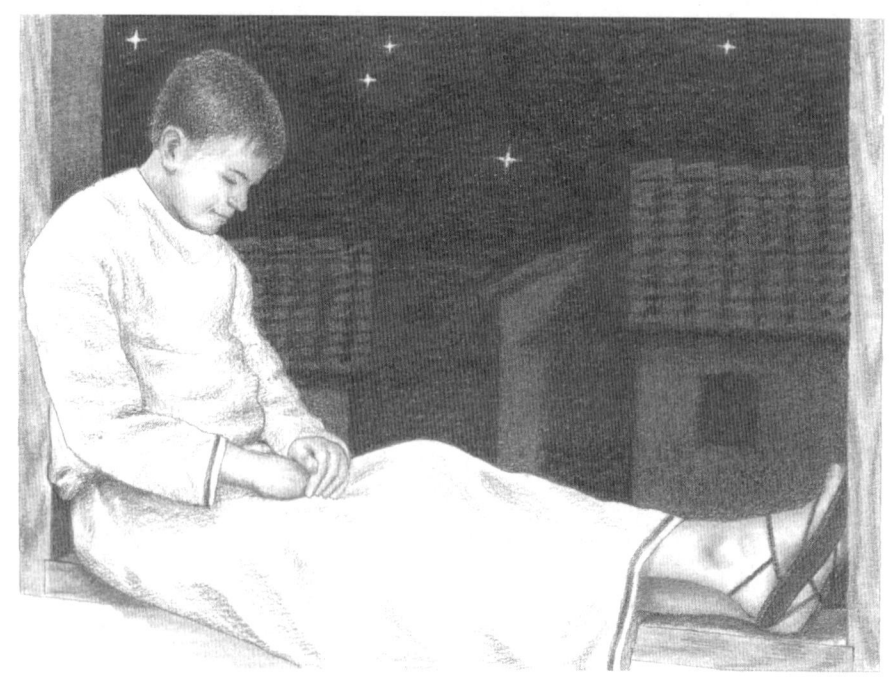

Ff

Felix could find no **fault** with Paul.

Felix

Acts 23, 24

Felix looked at the letter. Then he looked at the men who had given him the letter. These men had traveled all night. They had brought Paul to Felix. Why had they brought Paul? The letter said some men wanted to kill Paul. The men did not like Paul, because he was preaching about Jesus.

Paul's sister's son had heard these men talking. They were planning how they could kill Paul. Quickly he had gone and told the captain.

The captain had written this letter to the governor Felix. He had sent Paul to Felix. So Felix kept Paul safe until the day of his trial.

Many people came and said things against Paul. Felix listened. Then he wanted to hear what Paul had to say. Felix could not find any fault in Paul. But he wanted to please the Jews, so he kept Paul in prison.

Festus

Acts 24–26

Festus was the new governor after Felix. Felix had left Paul in prison. The people wanted Festus to punish Paul. Again they said many things against Paul. One day the king came to visit Festus. He wanted to see Paul. He wanted to hear what Paul had to say.

Festus commanded that Paul be brought from the prison. He said to the king, "This is the man the Jews want me to kill. But I cannot find any fault in him."

The king said to Paul, "You may speak for yourself." Paul gladly told the king about Jesus. The king listened. He said, "I almost believe the things Paul says about Jesus."

Paul said, "I wish everyone here would believe in Jesus."

Fortunatus

1 Corinthians 16:17

Fortunatus was a friend of Paul. He went to visit Paul while Paul was in Philippi. When Paul wrote a letter to the Christians at Corinth, he sent the letter to Corinth with Fortunatus. In the letter he wrote, "I am glad Fortunatus came to see me. He did good things for me while he was here. I may come to see you and stay over winter."

Gg

Gehazi wanted the **gifts**.

Gehazi

2 Kings 5

Gehazi was a servant to the prophet Elisha. Gehazi helped Elisha.

Someone was at the door. Elisha sent Gehazi to the door. Naaman had come from far away. He was sick. No one had been able to help him. Even the doctors could not heal him. He wanted Elisha to make him well.

Elisha sent Gehazi to tell Naaman what to do. Naaman obeyed and God healed him. How happy he was to be well again! He wanted to tell Elisha thank-you. He wanted to give him gifts.

Elisha said, "I do not want your gifts. It is God who made you well."

Naaman started home. Gehazi ran after him. He said, "Please give me your gifts. Elisha wants them after all." But that was not true. Gehazi wanted them for himself. Gehazi went home and hid the gifts.

But Elisha knew what Gehazi had done. He said to Gehazi, "Because you did this, you will have the sickness that Naaman had."

Gideon

Judges 6–8

Gideon was a man of God. Many people in Israel had forgotten God. They worshiped idols. God did not help them. He let their enemies make life hard for them.

The children of Israel were having a hard time. They were sorry they had forgotten God. They asked God to help them.

God sent an angel to Gideon. The angel said, "The Lord is with you, Gideon."

Gideon said, "If God is with us, why do our enemies rule over us?"

God told Gideon, "I will help you save Israel from your enemies. Tear down the altar of Baal. Build an altar to God."

Gideon obeyed God. Some men helped him. When they obeyed God, He helped them win the battle against their enemies. The children of Israel were free again!

Goliath

1 Samuel 17

Goliath was a very big man. He was a giant. Goliath and his people were enemies to Israel. Every day Goliath came to the children of Israel. He called, "Send me a man. We will fight. If he kills me, we will be your servants. But if I kill him, you will be our servants."

The children of Israel were afraid. They did not want to fight with that big man. Though David was a young man, he said to the king, "I will go. I will fight the giant. God will help me."

The king looked at David. He said, "You cannot fight the giant. He is a big man. He knows how to fight. You are just a youth."

David told the king, "God will help me kill the giant." So the king told David he could fight the giant.

When Goliath saw David, he was angry. He said, "Come, I will kill you." But David was not afraid. He did not run away. He ran to meet Goliath.

David said to Goliath, "You come to kill me with a sword. But I come to you in the name of the Lord. He will help me. Then everyone will know there is a God in Israel." Then David took a stone. He put it in his sling. He slung it at Goliath. The stone hit Goliath in the head. He fell down to the ground. David took Goliath's own sword and killed him.

Gamaliel

Acts 5:34–40; 22:3

Gamaliel was a great teacher. He taught school when Paul was a boy. Gamaliel sat on a low seat facing his students. A row of boys sat on the floor in front of him. Paul was one of those boys. Day after day they came to hear Gamaliel teach.

Gamaliel was a wise man. He taught many good things. He used the Bible for a textbook. Every day they studied the Old Testament law.

Hh

Hur and Aaron held up Moses' **hands**.

Hur

Exodus 17

Hur, Moses, and Aaron were standing at the top of the hill. They were watching the people. Some men had come to fight against Israel. Moses held up his hands. He prayed. He asked God to help Israel. The children of Israel were chasing the enemies away. Moses' arms were very tired. They felt heavy. Finally his arms fell by his side. Then the enemies turned and chased Israel. The children of Israel were running away from them.

Moses held up his hands again. Again the children of Israel were chasing their enemies. But Moses was very tired. Someone brought a stone for Moses to sit on. Aaron and Hur stood beside Moses. Hur held up his hand on one side. Aaron held up his hand on the other side. As long as Moses' hands were held up, the enemies could not hurt Israel. God helped Israel win the battle.

Hannah

1 Samuel 1

Hannah loved God. Every year she went to the temple. She went with her husband to offer sacrifices to God. But Hannah was not happy. She was sad because she did not have any children. Hannah wanted a baby very much.

One year when Hannah went to the temple, she asked God to give her a baby. She cried and she prayed. Eli saw her. He thought she was drunk. When Eli scolded her, she said, "No, I was praying to God because I am sad."

Eli said, "Go and be happy. God will answer your prayer."

Hannah believed Eli. God did answer her prayer. God gave Hannah a baby boy. She named him Samuel.

Hezekiah

2 Kings 20:1–11

Hezekiah was a good king. He helped the children of Israel. He tore down their idols and taught them to worship God.

Hezekiah became very sick. Isaiah the prophet came to visit him. He said, "God said that you must get ready to die. You will not get well." Hezekiah did not want to die. He turned his face to the wall. He cried and prayed to God.

Isaiah started home. He had not gone far when God spoke to him again. God said, "Go back. Tell Hezekiah I heard his prayer. I saw his tears. I will make him well." Hezekiah was so happy. He could hardly believe the good news. God did make him well!

Haman

Esther 5–7

Haman was a wicked man. He was proud. He wanted everyone to honor him. One day he saw a man who would not bow down to him. This made Haman angry. He thought of a wicked plan to kill this man and all his family.

Haman made a big, high gallows to hang the man who would not bow down to him.

But his plan did not work. The king said, "Hang Haman himself on the gallows that he made."

Haman died on the gallows that he had made to kill another man.

Ii

Isaac's servants dug a third well **instead** of fighting.

Isaac

Genesis 26:12–25

Isaac loved and obeyed God. God blessed him with flocks of sheep and herds of cattle. He had many servants to care for his animals.

Isaac's neighbors did not like that he had more riches than they had. The king of that place came to Isaac and said, "You go away from here. We do not want you to live near us."

So Isaac took his sheep and cattle and his servants and moved to another place. They went to a valley where Isaac's father, Abraham, had lived. There Abraham had dug wells to water his animals. Isaac would need much water for all his animals.

When they came to the valley where the wells had been, there was no water. Someone had filled the wells with dirt. But Isaac did not fuss. He told his servants to dig the dirt out. Soon they had a well overflowing with water. Now they could water their animals.

Their enemies came and fought with Isaac's servants. They said, "This is our water." So Isaac let them have the well, and he told his servants to dig another well.

Again the people came and fought for this well. But still Isaac did not fight back. He just let them have it.

Isaac told his servants to dig a third well. This time no one took it away from them. They had all the water they needed. God was pleased with Isaac.

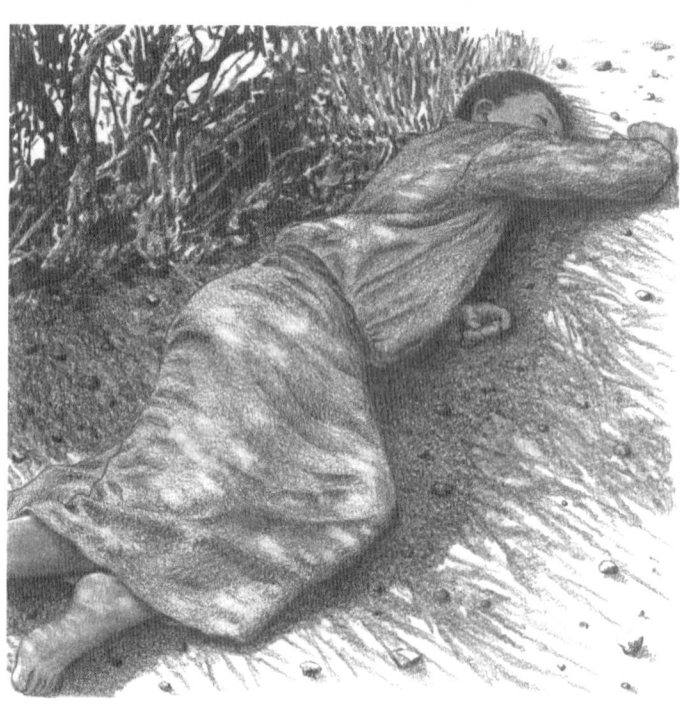

Ishmael

Genesis 21:12–21

Ishmael was hot. He was thirsty. He and his mother walked on and on. They did not know which way to go. Their water was all gone. The sun beat down on the hot, dry land. Ishmael was weak and faint. His mother was afraid he would die. She laid him down beside a little bush. She walked away and cried.

God saw her. He saw Ishmael. Suddenly Ishmael's mother heard a voice from heaven. The angel of God called her name. He showed her where there was water. How happy she was! Quickly she got some water and gave it to her son. God said, "I will make Ishmael a great nation."

Ichabod

1 Samuel 4

Ichabod was a tiny baby. He never knew his own mother. She died the day he was born. He never knew his father. He was killed in the war that same day. His grandpa died the same day too.

It was a sad time in Israel. The children of Israel had sinned. Now God did not help them. Their enemies came to fight against them. The enemies took the ark of God away. They killed many people.

Ichabod's grandpa was Eli. Eli was the priest. He was old and blind. He sat outside by the road, waiting. He was waiting to hear news about the war. Someone came running. He told Eli, "Many people in Israel were killed. Your two sons were killed. The enemies took the ark of God away." When Eli heard that the ark of God was taken, he fell over backward and died.

Ichabod's mother heard all this bad news. She heard that Ichabod's father was killed in the war. She said, "Call my baby Ichabod." The name Ichabod means that God was not helping Israel. Then she died.

Ittai

2 Samuel 15–18

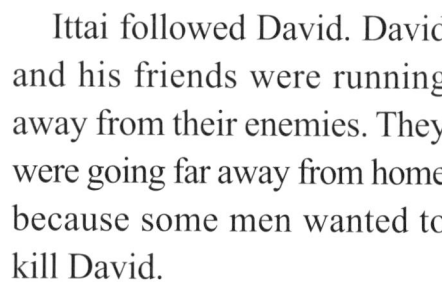

Ittai followed David. David and his friends were running away from their enemies. They were going far away from home because some men wanted to kill David.

David said to Ittai, "Why do you go with us? You are not one of us. You are a stranger. Go back home with your family."

But Ittai did not want to go home. He wanted to go with David. He wanted to help David. Ittai said, "No, I will go with you. I will help you even if I die!"

David let Ittai go with them. Ittai was faithful to David. Later David made Ittai one of his captains.

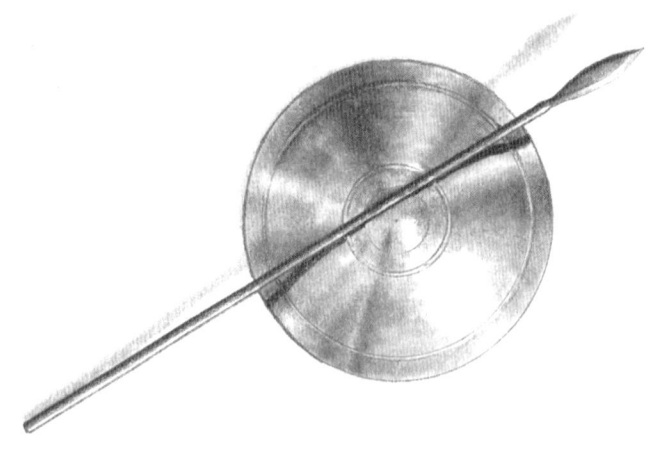

Jj

James and **John** follow Jesus.

James and John

Matthew 4:21, 22

James and John sat in the fishing boat with their father. They had been fishing all night. They had caught so many fish that their nets broke. Now they were mending the nets. They needed to fix the holes before they went fishing again.

Jesus was walking by the sea. He saw James and John in the boat. Jesus called to them, "Come and follow Me."

Right away they got up and followed Jesus. Day after day they went with Jesus. James and John wanted to hear Jesus preach and to see Him heal the sick. They learned many good things from Jesus.

Jacob

Genesis 28

Jacob walked on and on. He was going to his uncle Laban's house. It was a long way. He could not walk there in one day. The sun went down. It was getting very dark. Jacob found stones that he used for pillows. Jacob lay down to sleep.

That night Jacob had a strange dream. He saw a big ladder. The ladder reached up to heaven. Angels were going up and down on the ladder. The Lord was at the top of the ladder. The Lord said to Jacob, "I am the God of your father. I am with you. I will keep you."

Jacob awoke. He said, "The Lord is in this place, and I did not know it."

Jacob built an altar out of the stones he had used for his pillows and worshiped God there.

Jeremiah

Jeremiah 38

Jeremiah was a prophet of the Lord. He told the people God's words. The king's sons did not like God's words. They did not like Jeremiah. They caught him and put him down into a deep hole. They let him down, down, down with ropes. At the bottom Jeremiah sank into the deep mud. It was wet and dark. Jeremiah thought he would die there.

But God saw him. God took care of him. He sent Ebedmelech to help him out of the deep hole.

Ebedmelech took ropes and rags. He took some men along to help him. They went to the deep hole. Ebedmelech called to Jeremiah. Ebedmelech heard Jeremiah answer. They let the ropes and rags down to Jeremiah. Jeremiah put the ropes under his arms and put the rags between his arms and the ropes so the ropes would not hurt him. Carefully they pulled Jeremiah out of the hole. Up, up, up he came. How good it was to see light! How good it felt to be on dry ground and feel the warm, bright sunshine!

Now what do you think Jeremiah did when he was out of that deep, dark hole? Did he run away? Did he hide? No, he kept right on telling the people the words of God.

Jairus

Mark 5:22–43

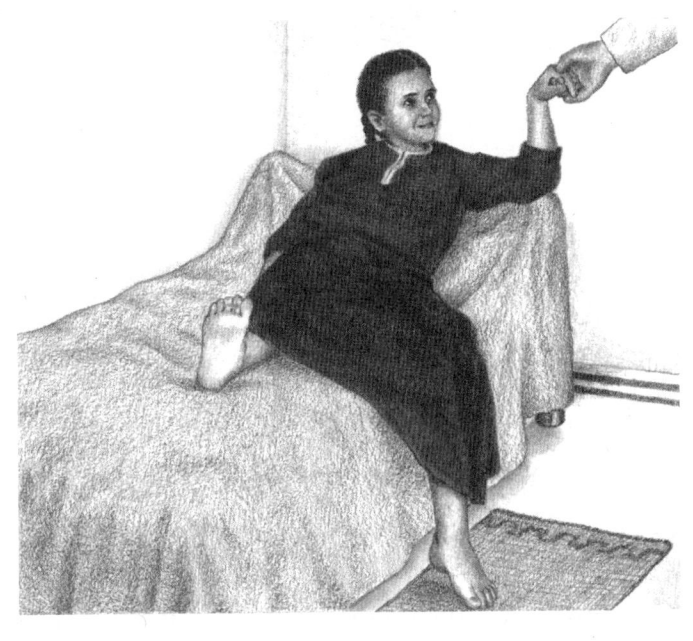

Jairus went to find Jesus. His little girl was sick. He wanted Jesus to come and make her well. Jairus saw many people. There was Jesus! He was talking to the people. He was healing the sick.

Jairus bowed down to Jesus. He said, "Come quickly. My little daughter is very sick. I am afraid she will die."

Jesus went with Jairus. But they could not go very fast. There were so many people. Some wanted to talk to Jesus. Some wanted Jesus to heal them.

Soon a man came. He said to Jairus, "Your little daughter is dead."

Jesus heard what the man said. Jesus said to Jairus, "Do not be afraid. I will make your little daughter well."

Jesus went with Jairus. The house was full of people. They were crying. Jesus told them to go out. He went in with the mother and father of the girl. He said to the girl, "Get up." She opened her eyes. She got up and walked. How happy Jairus was! His little daughter was alive and well.

 **Korah** was **killed** when the earth opened up.

Korah

Numbers 16

Korah wanted to be a great man. He wanted to be a leader. He did not like that God had chosen Moses to lead the children of Israel. He did not want to obey Moses. Korah talked to some other men. "We are as good as Moses," he said. "We could be just as good a leader as he."

Korah and his friends went to Moses. They said, "You think you are so great. We are just as good as you."

God was not pleased with Korah and his friends. He did not like what Korah and his friends did. God had chosen Moses to be the leader. He wanted the people to obey Moses.

God said to Moses, "Tell all the people to get away from these men. I will punish them." Some of the people obeyed Moses. They went away from Korah. Suddenly something very strange happened. The ground opened up where Korah and his friends were standing. They fell into the big hole. Their tents fell in. Then the ground closed up again.

Keturah

Genesis 25:1–4

Keturah was Abraham's new wife. Abraham was 137 years old when his first wife, Sarah, died. Then Abraham took Keturah for his wife. Now Abraham was not alone. Abraham was happy.

Abraham and Keturah lived in a tent. God gave them six sons. They were a happy family.

Kish

1 Samuel 9

Kish was a great man. He had big fields. He had many animals. One day he could not find his donkeys. They were lost.

Kish had a young son. His name was Saul. Kish called, "Saul, get up. Go out and find the donkeys."

Saul looked and looked. For two days he walked. He looked here and there. But he could not find the donkeys.

At last Saul decided, "I will go to Samuel. He is a man of God. I will ask him where to look for the donkeys. Maybe he can tell me where they are."

Saul went to Samuel. Samuel said, "Saul, do not worry about the donkeys. They are found. And now your father is looking for you."

Ll

Lazarus was raised to **life** by Jesus.

Lazarus

John 11

Lazarus lived with his sisters, Mary and Martha. They loved Jesus and Jesus loved them. Jesus often came to their house.

One day Lazarus became very sick. Mary and Martha sent someone to tell Jesus. They said, "Your friend Lazarus is sick." They hoped Jesus would come and make him well. But Jesus did not come right away. Lazarus became sicker. Then he died. How sad Mary and Martha were!

Someone said, "Jesus is coming!" Oh, how they wished He had come sooner! They thought, "Now it is too late."

Jesus walked over to the grave where Lazarus's body lay. He said, "Lazarus, come out." Lazarus became alive. He stood up. He walked. He talked. Everyone was surprised. Mary and Martha were happy to see their brother Lazarus alive again.

Levi

Luke 5:27–32

Levi helped collect tax money for the Roman rulers. The Jews did not like to pay taxes. They did not like the ones who collected the taxes. Levi sat at a table, taking taxes from the people. Jesus walked by. He saw Levi. Jesus said, "Levi, come and follow Me." Right away Levi followed Jesus. Levi made a feast for Jesus. Another name for Levi was Matthew. He wrote the Gospel of Matthew in our Bible.

Lydia

Acts 16:13–15

Lydia walked along with some of her friends. They were going down to the river. It was the Sabbath Day. They did not have a church house as we do. So every Sabbath Day, they went down to the river. There they kneeled down by the riverside and prayed to God.

Paul heard about their prayer meeting down by the riverside. Paul went down to the river. He taught them more about God and Jesus. Lydia listened. She believed what Paul said. Lydia believed and was saved.

Luke

Colossians 4:14

Luke was a doctor. He wrote two books in the Bible. He wrote the book of Luke. In this book he told stories about Jesus' life on earth.

Luke also wrote the book of Acts. In this book he tells stories about Peter and the other followers of Jesus. Sometimes Luke went with Paul on his travels and helped him.

Mm

Miriam watched over baby **Moses**.

Miriam

Exodus 2:1–10

    Miriam stood quietly by the river. She was watching the little basket as it bobbed up and down, up and down on the water at the edge of the river. Miriam's baby brother, Moses, was in that basket.

    The king had made a law. He said, "All the baby boys that are born to God's people must be killed." Moses' mother did not want her baby to be killed. So she made a little basket-boat and put baby Moses into it. Miriam watched to see what would happen. Soon the king's daughter came along. She saw the basket-boat. The king's daughter saw the baby in it, and she loved him. She said, "I will take him home to be my baby. But I need a nurse to take care of him."

    Miriam asked the king's daughter, "Shall I get a nurse for you?"

    She said, "Yes, go and get one."

    Quickly Miriam ran home and got her mother. Now no one would kill their baby. Moses' own mother could take care of him. She taught Moses to love and obey God.

Mahlon

Ruth 1

Mahlon was hungry. His father and mother were hungry. There was not enough food in the land of Israel. It had not rained for a long time, so it was very dry. Mahlon's family moved to the land of Moab. There they had food. But the people in the land of Moab did not know the true God. They worshiped idols. But Mahlon's father taught him to worship the one true God.

Then Mahlon's father died. Mahlon lived with his mother, Naomi. Later Mahlon married a girl in Moab. Her name was Ruth. Ruth's family worshiped idols. But Ruth learned to know the true God.

After a few years Mahlon died. Now Naomi and Ruth were both widows. They decided to go back to the land of Israel together.

Mephibosheth

2 Samuel 4

Mephibosheth was five years old. He did not understand what was happening. Why was everyone afraid? Why was everyone running away? Someone had come with news. Mephibosheth's father was killed in battle. His grandfather Saul was killed too. Saul's servants knew that everyone in Saul's house was in danger.

Mephibosheth's nurse picked him up and ran very fast. She was going to hide him where no one could find him. As she hurried, she let him fall. His feet were hurt. He was hurt so badly that he was crippled all his life. He could not run and play like other boys and girls. He was lame in both his feet.

Mary

Luke 2:1–7

Mary was very tired. She and Joseph had traveled for many miles. The ruler had made a law that everyone must be counted. He wanted to know how many people there were. They had to go to their hometown to be counted. Joseph and Mary were on their way to Bethlehem, their hometown. On and on they plodded.

There were many people in Bethlehem. Joseph tried to find a room for the night. But there was no room for them in the inn. Finally they went out to a stable. There they lay down to sleep. That night a wonderful thing happened! Baby Jesus was born. Mary was His mother. She laid Him in a manger for His bed.

Nn

Nicodemus came to Jesus at **night**.

Nicodemus

John 3:1–21

Nicodemus walked along in the dark. He was thinking. He wanted to talk to Jesus. Nicodemus was a ruler of the Jews. He and the other rulers taught the people. They told them the way to heaven. But they did not even know the way themselves. Nicodemus wanted to know.

That night Jesus taught Nicodemus how to be saved. Jesus said, "God loved the world so much that He sent His Son to die for everyone. If you believe in Me, you will have everlasting life."

Noah

Genesis 6–8

Noah loved God. He had three sons. He taught his sons to love and obey God. The people around them worshiped idols. They did not know the true God. They did not want to obey God.

One day God said to Noah, "Build a big boat. There will be a great flood. You and your family will be safe in the boat."

Noah believed God. He obeyed God. He and his sons built a big boat. Noah and his family went into the boat. When they were all in the boat, God shut the door. Then it began to rain. It rained for many days. Soon everything was covered with water. But Noah and his family were safe in the boat. They were saved because they obeyed God. We are safe too if we obey God.

Naboth

1 Kings 21

Naboth was a godly man. He loved and obeyed God. Naboth's land was right beside King Ahab's house. Naboth planted long rows of grapes on his land.

The king looked out his window. How beautiful Naboth's land looked! "I wish I had that land," he thought. So he walked over to Naboth's house. "Sell me your land," he said. "It is close to my house. I want it for my garden."

"No," said Naboth. "I cannot do that. This land belonged to my father. It belonged to his fathers before him. Long ago God told us, 'You shall not sell the land that your fathers gave you.' I cannot sell this land."

King Ahab was upset. His wife was upset. They wanted that land with grapes. They got some men to tell lies about Naboth. Then they took him out and killed him.

God saw what Ahab did. God said to Elijah, "Go and tell Ahab he will be punished for what he did."

Nehemiah

Nehemiah 1, 2

Nehemiah served the king. Every day he gave the king his drink. One day the king asked, "Nehemiah, why are you so sad? You were never like this before."

Nehemiah had been sad for a few days. He had cried, and he did not eat. Now he prayed to God to help him know how to answer the king. He said, "I am sad because I had news from the land of my fathers. They are poor. Their walls are broken down. Their enemies trouble them."

The king and queen listened. "Do you want to go and help them?" they asked. "We will help you. But we want you to come back." The king let him go to help build the walls of the city. He even gave Nehemiah some things he needed for building. How happy Nehemiah was then!

Oo

Obadiah was the king's **officer**.

Obadiah

1 Kings 18:1–16

Obadiah worked for the king. The land was very dry. One day the king said to Obadiah, "Go and walk over the land. Look for some green grass for the horses. If we do not find some grass, they will all die."

Obadiah walked and walked. He met Elijah. Elijah said, "Go and tell the king that I am here."

Obadiah was afraid. He did not want to tell the king. He said, "If you are not here when the king comes, then he will kill me. Don't you know the king and his wife are angry at you? They want to kill you. They have killed many of the prophets of the Lord. Didn't you hear how I hid one hundred of the Lord's prophets in a cave? Every day I took them bread and water. I hid them from the king. I took care of them so they would not die."

Elijah said, "I will stay here and talk to the king." So Obadiah went and told the king. God took care of Elijah so the king could not hurt him.

Og

Deuteronomy 3:1–5, 11

Og was a king. He ruled over sixty cities with big walls around them. He lived in the land that God had promised to give to the children of Israel. God told Joshua to lead the children of Israel into the land of Canaan. God said, "Do not be afraid. I will give you this land."

King Og went out to fight against Israel. He was big and strong. He was a giant. The Bible tells us that his bed was more than thirteen feet long and six feet wide. King Og thought he could win the battle. But God helped the children of Israel. King Og was killed. God gave his land to the children of Israel. They took the walled cities. They lived in the land that God gave them.

Obed

Ruth 4

Obed was a tiny baby. He lay in the arms of his grandma. Oh, how she loved little Obed! Can you guess who his grandma was? Her name was Naomi. Do you remember Ruth? Ruth went back to the land of Israel with Naomi. Now God gave Ruth this dear little baby. She called him Obed.

When Obed was a big man, he had some children and grandchildren. Who do you think his grandson was? One of his grandsons was David, the shepherd boy, who later became King David.

Onesimus

Philemon

Onesimus was far away from home. He had not wanted to work for his master. So he ran away, far away to a place called Rome. There he met Paul. Paul was in prison in Rome. Onesimus loved Paul. He did many nice things for him. He tried to make Paul comfortable and to give him the things he needed.

Paul loved this kind young man. He taught him about God's love. He told him about Jesus and taught him how to be saved. Onesimus believed what Paul said. He believed in Jesus. He became a Christian.

Onesimus knew he should go back to his master. He must make things right with him. Onesimus did not want to leave Paul. Paul did not want him to leave either. But now Onesimus was a Christian. He wanted to do what was right.

Paul sent a letter with Onesimus to his master. He asked his master to be kind to Onesimus. Paul also said he would like to have Onesimus for a helper.

Pp

Peter was put in **prison**.

Peter

Acts 5:17–29

Peter was busy teaching the people about Jesus. Many people had come to hear him preach. This made the rulers angry. They said, "More people are following Peter than are following us." They did not like that. They caught Peter and put him in prison. They locked the doors. "Now," they thought, "that will stop Peter's preaching."

But God had other plans for Peter. That night God sent an angel to the prison. He opened the prison door. He led Peter out. Then the angel said, "Go back and teach the people the words of life."

The next morning the rulers came to the prison. They unlocked the prison door. How surprised they were when they looked inside! The room was empty! Peter was not there! "How could he get out?" they wondered. The door was still locked.

Someone came and told them that Peter was in the temple, teaching the people about Jesus again.

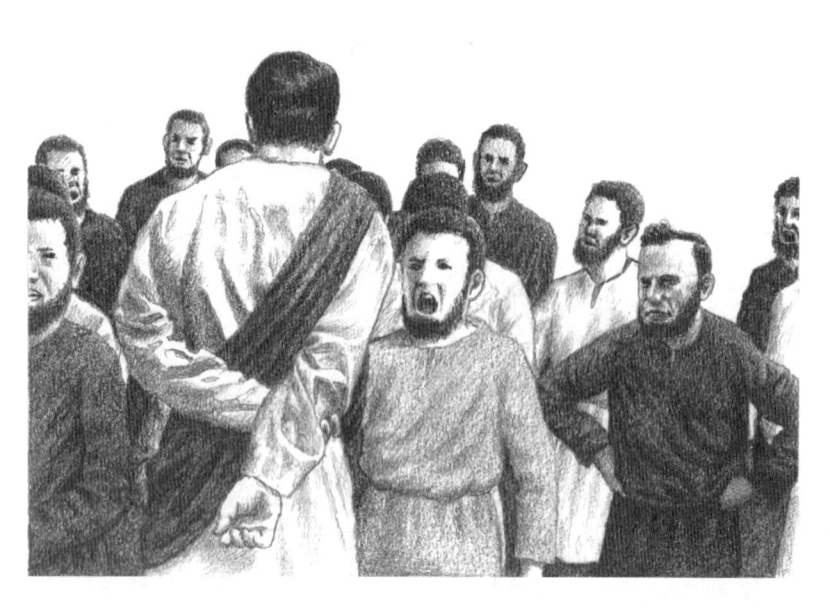

Pilate

Matthew 27

Pilate was a ruler of the Jews. Some men had brought Jesus to Pilate. They wanted Pilate to kill Jesus. Pilate talked to Jesus. Then he talked to the people. He said, "I do not find any fault in this Man."

The angry people shouted, "Crucify Him! Crucify Him!"

Pilate asked, "Why? What evil has He done?" But no one could say any wrong that Jesus had done. Pilate did not want to kill a good man. The people became very angry. So Pilate let them have their own way.

Pilate's soldiers led Jesus out and nailed Him to the cross. Jesus died. He was buried. But in three days He arose from the dead! He is alive. He is in heaven now.

Philip

Acts 8:26–39

Philip was walking along a desert road. God had told him to go this way. He did not know why. Then up ahead he saw a horse and chariot. A man was riding in the chariot. As he came nearer, Philip could hear him reading. He was reading the Bible. Philip ran up to the chariot. He asked the man, "Do you understand what you are reading?"

"No," said the man, "I need someone to teach me." He asked Philip to come up and sit in the chariot with him. Philip taught him about Jesus. The man listened. Then he said, "I believe that Jesus is the Son of God." He became a follower of Jesus.

Priscilla

Acts 18

Priscilla was Aquila's wife. They loved God. While they were working, they would tell other people about God.

Paul came to the town where Aquila and Priscilla lived. They were making tents. Paul knew how to make tents too and worked for them.

For a while he lived with Aquila and Priscilla. Paul had come to this town to preach. When he was not preaching, he helped Aquila and Priscilla make tents.

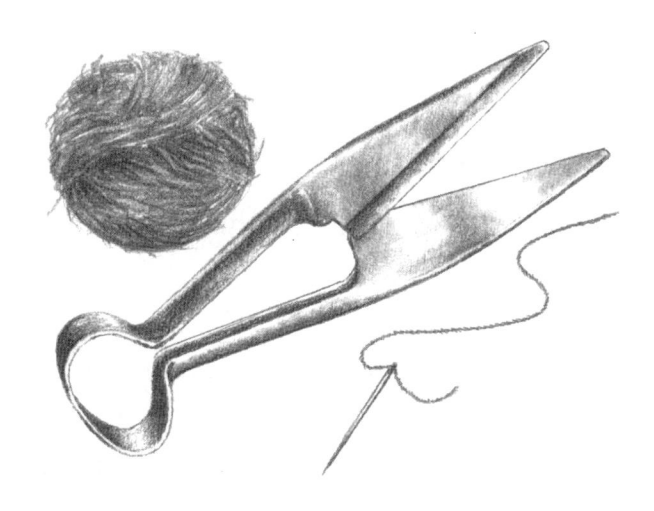

Qq

Quartus quietly served God.

Quartus

Romans 16:23

Quartus was a Christian. Paul calls him a brother. He meant a brother in Christ. The Bible calls people who follow Jesus brothers. They are all God's children. They are all in God's family.

The Bible does not tell us much about Quartus. But the important thing is that he served the Lord. We do not have to do great things. We can quietly serve the Lord. We can obey Him.

Jesus said, "If you give a cup of cold water to a little one in My name, you will have a reward."

Do you want to serve the Lord? Would you like to do something for Jesus? Do something nice for others!

Queen of Sheba

1 Kings 10:1–13

The Queen of Sheba had heard about King Solomon. She had heard how God had blessed him with riches and great wisdom. She could hardly believe all the things that she had heard. She wanted to know if it was really true. She wanted to ask him some very hard questions. She wanted to see his beautiful palace.

The Queen of Sheba lived in a land far away. She got her camels ready. She was going to see King Solomon. She took many rich gifts to give to this great king.

She saw the beautiful house that he had built. She saw his riches and the good food on his table. She saw the fine clothes he had to wear. He had many servants. He was able to answer all her questions.

How surprised she was! She said, "I could not believe all the things I heard about you. Now I believe because I have seen it with my own eyes. I had not heard even half of your greatness."

We do not know the name of the Queen of Sheba. But many years later, Jesus praised this queen for her faith in God.

Rr

Rahab put a red **rope** in her window.

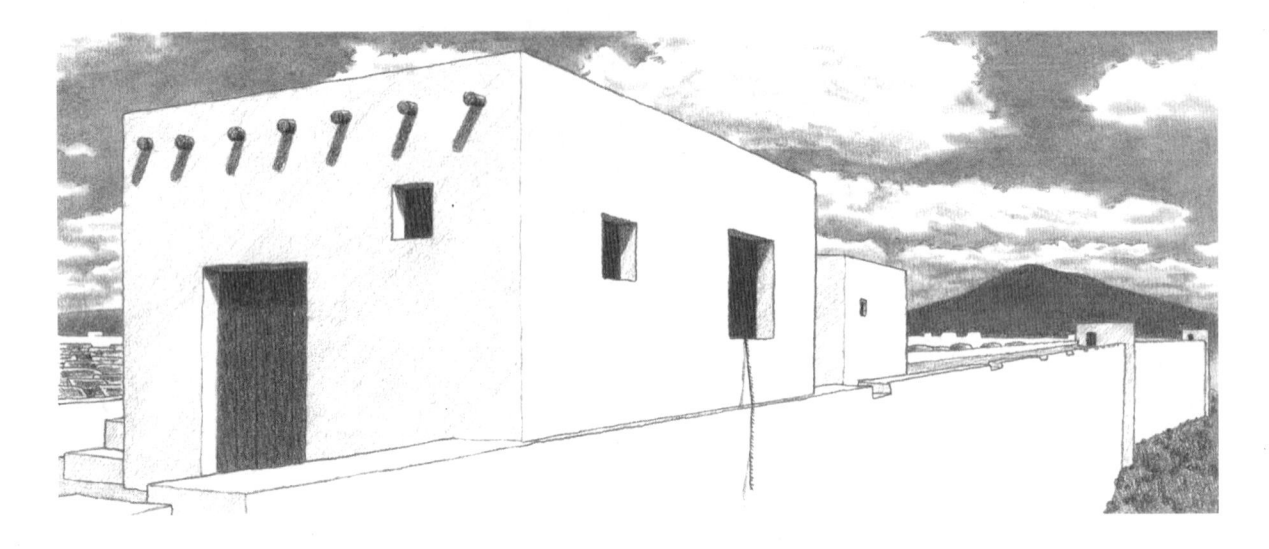

Rahab

Joshua 2

Rahab lived in the city of Jericho. There were thick, high walls around the city. Rahab's house was built on this wall.

Everyone in Jericho was afraid. The children of Israel were coming near their city. They had heard about all the wonderful things God had done for Israel before.

Joshua sent two men into the city to look it over. The king of the city heard that two men had come. He tried to find them. He wanted to kill them.

Rahab took the two men up onto the roof of her house. She hid them there and covered them with stalks of flax. That night she let them down over the wall with a rope.

The men told Rahab, "Hang this red rope in your window. When we come back to take the city, we will save you and your family alive because of your kindness to us." Because Rahab believed in God, she and her family were saved.

Reuben

Genesis 37

Reuben and his brothers were taking care of their father Jacob's sheep. They had been away from home for many days. One day Jacob sent Joseph to see how his brothers were doing. The brothers hated Joseph. They knew their father loved him most.

When they saw Joseph coming, one brother said, "Let's kill him."

"No," said Reuben. "Let's put him into that pit nearby." The brothers thought that was a good plan. But Reuben was planning to pull him out when his brothers were not looking so that Joseph could go home. So they put poor Joseph down into the pit.

While Reuben was away, some men came by. The brothers took Joseph out of the pit and sold him to these men.

When Reuben came back, the brothers were not around. He quickly went to help Joseph out of the pit. He wanted to let him run home to his father. But Joseph was no longer in the pit. Reuben asked his brothers, "Where is Joseph?"

The brothers said, "We sold him to some men. They took him far away." Reuben was sad because of what his brothers had done.

God was with Joseph. Many years later Joseph said to his brothers, "You meant it for evil, but God meant it for good." God had a plan for Joseph.

Rehoboam

1 Kings 12:1–20

Rehoboam was Solomon's son. After King Solomon died, Rehoboam was made king. He was young. He did not know how to rule the people. He called the old men who had helped his father. He asked, "What shall I do? How shall I rule the people?"

The old men answered, "Be good to the people. Treat them kindly. Then they will be your servants. They will do whatever you tell them."

Next Rehoboam called the young men. He asked them, "What do you think? How shall I rule the people?"

The young men answered, "Tell them, 'I will make you work hard. I will punish you more cruelly than my father did.'"

Rehoboam was young. He was proud and selfish. He liked what the young men said. He was not kind to the people. He told them he would make them work very hard. Many of the people went away from him. They made another king for themselves. Only a few people followed Rehoboam.

Rhoda

Acts 12

Rhoda and some other Christians were at Mary's house. They had gone there to pray for Peter. The king had put Peter in prison. He was planning to kill Peter the next day.

Rhoda listened. What did she hear?

Knock. Knock. Knock.

She heard it again. Someone was at the gate. Rhoda went to answer the knock. Then she heard Peter's voice. She was so surprised that she did not even open the gate! She ran to tell the others. "Peter is at the gate!"

They could not believe it. All this time Peter kept on knocking. The others hurried to the gate. How surprised they were to see him there!

Peter said, "I was sleeping in the prison with chains on my hands. Soldiers were guarding me. An angel came and touched me. He said, 'Get up quickly. Get dressed.' My chains fell off. I followed the angel. We went outside. The big iron gate was locked, but it opened by itself. At first I thought I was dreaming. When we were outside, I knew it was true. Then the angel left. I came here!"

Ss

Saul **s**at in a basket, and they let him down outside the wall.

Saul

Acts 9:23–25

Saul loved God. He preached boldly. Day after day he taught the people about God. Many Jews believed. This made the rulers angry. They wanted to hurt Saul. They guarded the gates. They planned to catch Saul when he went out of the city.

But the Christians heard about it. They loved Saul. They wanted to help him get away. They hid Saul until it was dark. That night they took Saul to the city wall. They took a big basket and some strong ropes. Saul sat in the basket. Then they let him down outside the city wall. Slowly and carefully they let the basket down until Saul's feet touched the ground. The guards could not see them. They were still waiting at the gates to catch Saul. God helped Saul to get away safely.

Later Saul was called Paul. He traveled far to tell many people about God. He also wrote many letters to Christians. Some of Paul's letters are part of our Bible today.

Shadrach

Daniel 3

Shadrach was going to a strange land. An enemy king had come to Jerusalem. He had taken many people from their homes. On and on they walked, day after day. Each night they stopped to rest by the roadside. They were being taken far away. In this group of people were Shadrach, Daniel, and some of their friends. They were all captives.

At last they came to a big city. Here the people worshiped idols. They did not know the true God. But Shadrach and his friends did not forget God.

The king in this land made a big idol. He said, "Everyone must bow down and worship my idol. Anyone who does not worship the idol will be thrown into the fire." Shadrach and his friends would not bow down and worship the idol.

The king became angry and threw them into the fire. But God took care of them. The fire did not hurt them. Then the king was afraid. He said, "Come out of the fire. Now I know there is no god like your God."

Simeon

Luke 2:25–35

Simeon was old. He was a godly man. He read the Bible. God had shown Simeon that soon He would send His Son to be the Saviour of the world. Oh, how Simeon wanted to see the Saviour before he died. Every day he waited and hoped to see the Son of God.

When Jesus was eight days old, His mother and Joseph took Him to the temple to offer a sacrifice.

Old Simeon was in the temple. He saw Joseph and Mary coming with baby Jesus. He knew this was Jesus, the Son of God. He knew that Jesus would be the Saviour of the world. Simeon took baby Jesus in his arms and said, "Now I am ready to die. Now I have seen the one who came to bring salvation to the world." Joseph and Mary were surprised at the things that he said.

Stephen

Acts 6, 7

Stephen was one of the seven deacons. He helped the poor. He gave them things they needed. Sometimes he preached to the people.

Once while he was preaching, some people became very angry. They were angry because Stephen told them, "This Jesus whom you killed is the Son of God." Stephen said, "Your fathers were stubborn; they killed the prophets. You are stubborn like your fathers. You do not obey God."

When the people heard these things, they held their ears shut. They did not want to hear any more. They ran up to Stephen. They caught him and took him out of the city. They threw stones at him until he died.

Before he died, Stephen prayed, "Lord, forgive them."

Tt

Terah and his son Abram lived in **t**ents.

Terah

Genesis 11:25–32

Terah was Abram's father. Terah worshiped idols. But Abram worshiped the living God. We do not know how Abram learned to know the true God. But it could be that he had heard the story from Noah's sons. Abram loved and obeyed God.

One day God called Abram. He said, "Get out of this land. Go away from Terah's house. I will show you where to go. I will bless you. I will make you a great nation." Abram obeyed God. He did not want to worship Terah's idols.

Tobiah

Nehemiah 4

Tobiah watched the Jews. They were building a big wall. "Ho, ho, ho," Tobiah laughed. "Your wall is so weak it will not stand. Even if a fox went up on your wall, it would fall down!"

That really was not true. Tobiah was making fun of them. He wanted to make the Jews afraid. He wanted to make them stop building.

Nehemiah was helping the Jews build the new wall. He knew what to do when Tobiah tried to stop them. He prayed to God and God helped them. Everyone worked hard. God blessed their work. Soon the big, strong wall was finished. Tobiah could not stop them.

Thomas

John 20:19–29

Thomas was one of Jesus' disciples. Day after day he had followed Jesus. But now what? Jesus was dead. This made Thomas very sad.

The other disciples gathered together in a room. They closed the door. Thomas was not with them. They were talking about Jesus. How they missed Jesus.

Suddenly Jesus was in the room with them. He helped them understand why He died and rose again. He did this to take away the sins of the world, He told them. Now He is the Saviour of the world.

After Jesus left, the disciples found Thomas. They were very happy. They had seen Jesus. They told Thomas, "Jesus is alive!"

Thomas could not believe what he was hearing. Thomas said, "I cannot believe that Jesus is alive. I will not believe it till I see Him with my own eyes."

The next time the disciples were together, Thomas was with them. Again Jesus came and talked with them. This time Thomas saw Jesus. Now he believed. Thomas said, "My Lord and my God!"

Timothy

2 Timothy 1; Acts 16:1

Timothy grew up in a wicked city. His father did not worship the true God. But his mother and his grandmother did. They taught Timothy to love and obey God.

When Timothy was a young man, he met Paul. Paul loved this young man. He taught him more about God. Paul said, "Timothy, my son, be strong. Study the Word of God. Pray. Preach the Word. Your mother had faith in God. Your grandmother had faith in God. You have faith in God. Now teach other people about Jesus. Teach them to trust in the living God." Timothy was a young preacher. He taught other people to love and obey God.

Uu

Urbane was **used** by God to help Paul.

Urbane

Romans 16:9

Urbane was Paul's helper. We do not know very much about Urbane. His name is found only once in the Bible. We may think, "He must not have been very important." But look what Paul calls him in the Bible: "My helper in Christ." Paul was a great preacher. God used Urbane to help Paul.

Do you know what Jesus said about helping others? Jesus said that if we do something for others, we do it for Him. Think about that! Would you like to do something for Jesus? Would you like to help Him?

Remember Urbane! He was a helper. You can be a helper too. Who can you help? You can help your mother. You can help your father. You can help your sisters and brothers. You can help others.

Uzza

1 Chronicles 13

Uzza and his brother walked along beside the new cart. David and all Israel were happy. They were singing with all their might. Do you know why everyone was so happy? They were bringing the ark of God back home. They had built a new cart. They had put the ark of God on the new cart. Cows were pulling the cart.

The road was rough. Suddenly the cart shook. Uzza quickly put his hand out to hold the ark. God had told the people, "No one but the priests should touch the ark." God had told them to carry it with poles on their shoulders. This is the way they should have brought the ark back. It should not have been set on a cart.

When Uzza put his hand on the ark, God was not pleased. They were not obeying God. Uzza died right there.

Uzziah

2 Chronicles 26

Uzziah was sixteen years old when his father died. Uzziah's father had been the king. Now all the people came together to make young Uzziah the king.

While he was young, Uzziah listened to the prophet. He obeyed God. As long as he obeyed God, God helped him do great things. When enemies came to fight, God helped him win. He built towers. He dug wells and had nice farms. He had many animals.

When he became very great, Uzziah became proud. Now he did not obey God. Uzziah burned incense to God. Only the priests were allowed to burn incense.

Some priests talked to Uzziah. They said, "You are disobeying God. You should not do this." Uzziah did not want to listen to them. He became angry.

God punished him with a sickness called leprosy. King Uzziah was a leper until the day he died.

Vv

Vashti was **very** beautiful.

Vashti

Esther 1

Vashti was a very beautiful woman. She was the queen. The king made a great feast. He made the feast for all the men in his palace. The feast lasted for seven days. That was a long time to have a feast. Every day they had good things to eat. They had wine to drink.

The last day the king decided to do something very special. What do you think he did? He sent a servant to call the queen. He wanted all the men to see his beautiful queen Vashti.

Queen Vashti was also having a feast. She had invited all the women in the palace to her feast. She did not want to leave her feast. She did not want to go to the king's feast. She said, "I will not go."

Queen Vashti did not obey the king. He did not like that. He asked the men at his feast, "What shall I do to the queen? She did not obey me."

They said, "Do not let her be queen anymore. Find another queen." That is just what the king did.

Ww

"**W**e all are the **work** of thy hand."

We

Psalm 100

"We are his people, and the sheep of his pasture." God made us and we belong to Him.

We are part of God's plan. He loves us and wants us to believe in Him. Jesus said, "He that believeth on me hath everlasting life." God wants all of us to believe in Jesus and have everlasting life.

God made us. We belong to Him. God loves us. We love Him because He first loved us.

The children of Israel said, "All that the Lord has said, we will do."

We also should say, "All that the Lord has said, we will do."

Xx

Xerxes had a son named **Artaxerxes**.

Xerxes

Esther 1, 2

Xerxes was the Greek name for Ahasuerus. King Ahasuerus was king when Esther was made queen. King Ahasuerus was very kind to the Jews because he loved Queen Esther. He helped the Jews when their enemies tried to hurt them.

King Xerxes (Ahasuerus) had a son named Artaxerxes. His son Artaxerxes was also a king. The two kings, Xerxes and Artaxerxes, were not God's people, but God used them to help the children of Israel.

King Artaxerxes was king in the land where Nehemiah was taken as a captive. Nehemiah served the king. One day the king learned that Nehemiah was sad because the walls of Jerusalem were broken down. He told Nehemiah to take people with him and build the broken-down walls. He even gave him wood from his own forests to help with the building.

The children of Israel built the wall in fifty-two days. They were very happy when the wall was finished.

Yy

<u>Y</u>e are my friends. <u>Y</u>e means **you**.

You

John 15:14

You are one of God's children. God loves you. He wants you to love Him. Jesus said, "Ye are my friends, if ye do whatsoever I command you."

We have many stories in the Bible about God's people. Did you know the Bible talks about you?

One day mothers and fathers brought their children to Jesus. Some of the people thought they were too much bother to Jesus. But Jesus said, "Let the children come to Me." Jesus laid His hands on the children.

God made you. He wants you to praise Him. You can praise God by being thankful. You have many, many things to thank God for—food, clothing, your homes, safety, good health. You can praise God by being cheerful and kind. You can praise God when you sing. We love to praise God because He does so many wonderful things for us!

Jesus said, "I am going back to heaven. I will make a place for you. I will come again and take you to heaven. You can live in heaven with Me."

Zz

Zacchaeus was **zealous**.

Zacchaeus

Luke 19:1–10

Zacchaeus ran ahead of the people. He saw a tree beside the road. Quickly he climbed up the tree. He sat on a branch, looking down at the people. Jesus was coming this way. Many people were walking with Jesus.

Zacchaeus wanted to see Jesus. He was a little man. He was so short that he could not see over the heads of the people. Now he sat on the branch, waiting. Jesus was coming closer. When Jesus came to the tree where Zacchaeus was, He looked up. He said, "Zacchaeus, come down. I want to come to your house."

How surprised Zacchaeus must have been! But he was happy too! He was very glad to see Jesus. Now he could talk to Him. Jesus was even coming to his house. That day Zacchaeus became a follower of Jesus.

Zipporah

Exodus 2:15–22

Zipporah and her six sisters took care of their father's sheep. At the end of the day, they would lead the sheep to a well. There they got water for their sheep to drink. Often other shepherds came and chased their sheep away. The others let their own sheep drink first. They were very unkind.

Zipporah and her sisters had come to get water for their sheep. It was late, and they were tired. Would they need to wait until the unkind shepherds went away? But today something was different. A strange man was sitting at the well. His name was Moses. When the unkind shepherds came, they tried again to chase away Zipporah's sheep. Moses helped Zipporah and her sisters. He made the unkind shepherds wait.

Moses went to Zipporah's house. He worked for her father. Zipporah became Moses' wife. This was the same Moses who led the children of Israel out of Egypt.

Ziba

2 Samuel 9

Ziba had been Saul's servant. After Saul was killed in battle, David was made king. David called Ziba. He asked, "Is there anyone of Saul's family who is still living?" David remembered Saul's son Jonathan. He had loved Jonathan very much. Long ago he had promised to be kind to Jonathan and his family as long as he lived. Now David wanted to know if there was still anyone in Jonathan's family who was alive so that he could show kindness to them.

Ziba said, "Yes, one of Jonathan's sons is still alive. His name is Mephibosheth. He is lame in his feet."

David said, "Bring him to me. He will eat at my table as one of my sons." David gave Mephibosheth all the land that belonged to his father, Jonathan. He told Ziba and his fifteen sons to take care of the land for Mephibosheth.

Zacharias

Luke 1

Zacharias was a priest. Today was his turn to burn incense on the altar in the temple. No one but the priests were allowed to do this.

The priests went inside the holy place. Many people worshiped God outside. They worshiped and waited. This day they waited a long time. The priests did not usually stay so long. They wondered why Zacharias did not come out.

An angel had come to Zacharias. He said, "God sent me to tell you that you and your wife will have a baby boy. Call his name John."

That was hard for Zacharias to believe. He said, "I am old. My wife is old. How can this be?"

The angel said, "Because you did not believe, you will not be able to talk until your baby is born." When Zacharias came out of the temple, he could not talk.

At last Zacharias and his wife had a baby boy. They called him John. After that, Zacharias was able to talk again.

Questions and Answers

A.

1. What did God ask Abraham to do?
    God told Abraham to go away from his father's house.

2. Who was the first man?
    Adam was the first man.

3. Moses' brother was a priest. What was his name?
    His name was Aaron.

4. What kind deed did Abigail do?
    Abigail gave food to some hungry people.

B.

5. What did Baruch do for Jeremiah?
    Baruch wrote Jeremiah's words in a book.

6. Why did Balaam want to go to the king when God said "no"?
    Balaam wanted the money.

7. What strange thing did King Belshazzar see?
    King Belshazzar saw a hand writing on the wall.

8. What did blind Bartimaeus want Jesus to do?
    Bartimaeus wanted Jesus to heal his eyes so he could see.

C.

9. Why did Joshua and Caleb think they were able to take the good land?
    Caleb said, "The Lord will help us."

10. What message did Cushi take to David?
    Cushi said to David, "Your enemies are dead."

11. Who told Cleopas that the Bible says Jesus will give His life and rise again?
    Jesus told Cleopas, "The Bible says Jesus will give His life and rise again."

12. What did Peter tell Cornelius and his friends?
    Peter told Cornelius and his friends, "Jesus died to save people from their sins. Whoever believes in Jesus will be saved."

D.

13. Who made clothes for the poor?
    Dorcas made clothes for the poor.

14. Who helped Deborah fight Israel's enemies?
    Barak helped Deborah fight Israel's enemies.

15. How did God keep the lions from hurting Daniel?
    God sent an angel to shut the lions' mouths.

16. What work did Demetrius do?
    Demetrius made little silver temples.

E.

17. Who was the first woman?
    Eve was the first woman.

18. Where did God tell Elijah to hide?
    God told Elijah to hide by a brook.

19. What did Ezra want to do at Jerusalem?
    Ezra wanted to teach the people all God's laws.

20. What happened to Eutychus one night when Paul was preaching?
    Eutychus fell from a window on the third floor.

F.

21. Why was Paul sent to Felix?

    Paul was sent to Felix to keep him safe from men who wanted to kill him.

22. What did Paul tell Festus?

    Paul told Festus about Jesus.

23. What did Fortunatus do for Paul?

    Fortunatus carried Paul's letter to Corinth.

G.

24. Who taught Paul in school?

    Gamaliel taught Paul in school.

25. Who was Elisha's servant?

    Gehazi was Elisha's servant.

26. What did God tell Gideon to do?

    God told Gideon, "Tear down the altar of Baal. Build an altar to God."

27. Why did young David think he could kill the giant Goliath?

    David knew God would help him.

H.

28. Who held up Moses' hands when he was tired?

    Hur and Aaron held up Moses' hands.

29. What was Hannah praying for?

    Hannah was praying for a baby.

30. What good things did Hezekiah do for Israel?

    He tore down their idols. He taught them to worship God.

31. What happened with the gallows that Haman made?

    Haman was hanged on the gallows he had made.

I.

32. Why did Isaac's servants have to dig three wells?
    Their enemies fought to have the wells for themselves.

33. Why did Ishmael's mother lay him down beside a bush and walk away?
    Ishmael's mother was afraid he would die.

34. What sad thing happened the day Ichabod was born?
    Ichabod's mother, father, and grandpa all died the day he was born.

35. Why were David and his friends and Ittai running away from home?
    David and his friends and Ittai were running away because some men wanted to kill David.

J.

36. Who were the two brothers who left their fishing boat to follow Jesus?
    James and John left their fishing boat to follow Jesus.

37. What did Jacob see in a dream one night?
    Jacob dreamed that he saw a ladder that reached up to heaven.

38. What did Jeremiah do after he was pulled out of the deep hole?
    Jeremiah kept on telling the people the words of God.

39. Why did Jairus want to find Jesus?
    Jairus wanted Jesus to heal his little girl.

K.

40. What happened to Korah when he did not want to obey Moses?
    God punished Korah when the earth opened and he fell in.

41. Who was Keturah?
    Keturah was Abraham's wife after Sarah died.

42. What had Kish, Saul's father, lost?
    Kish had lost his donkeys.

L.

43. Why did Mary and Martha send for Jesus to come?
    Mary and Martha sent for Jesus because Lazarus was sick.

44. What was Levi's other name?
    Levi was also called Matthew.

45. What was Lydia doing down by the river?
    Lydia went to a prayer meeting down by the river.

46. Who was the doctor who wrote two books in the Bible?
    Luke was the doctor who wrote two books in the Bible.

M.

47. Why was Miriam hiding by the river?
    Miriam was watching her baby brother Moses.

48. Why did Mahlon and his family move to the land of Moab?
    Mahlon and his family moved to the land of Moab because it was very dry in the land of Israel.

49. Who was crippled the rest of his life because his nurse let him fall?
    Mephibosheth was crippled for life because his nurse let him fall.

50. Who was the mother of Jesus?
    Mary was the mother of Jesus.

N.

51. Who did Nicodemus want to talk to at night?
    Nicodemus wanted to talk to Jesus.

52. Why were Noah and his family saved when the world was destroyed with a flood?
    Noah and his family were saved because they obeyed God.

53. Why was King Ahab upset with Naboth?
    King Ahab was upset because Naboth would not sell his land.

54. Why was Nehemiah sad when he served the king his drink?
　　Nehemiah was sad because the land of his fathers was troubled by enemies.

O.

55. What brave deed did Obadiah do for some of God's prophets?
　　Obadiah hid one hundred of God's prophets in a cave and fed them.

56. Over how many walled cities did Og rule?
　　Og ruled over sixty walled cities.

57. Who was Obed's grandson?
　　King David was Obed's grandson.

58. Why did Onesimus go back to his master?
　　Onesimus was a Christian. He wanted to do what was right.

P.

59. Who helped Peter get out of prison?
　　An angel helped Peter get out of prison.

60. What did the Jews want Pilate to do with Jesus?
　　The Jews wanted Pilate to crucify Jesus.

61. What was the man in the chariot reading when Philip saw him?
　　The man in the chariot was reading the Bible when Philip saw him.

62. What work did Aquila, Priscilla, and Paul do?
　　Aquila, Priscilla, and Paul made tents.

Q.

63. What important thing did Quartus do?
　　Quartus served the Lord.

64. What did the Queen of Sheba say after she saw King Solomon?
　　The Queen of Sheba said, "I had not heard even half of your greatness."

R.

65. Where did Rahab hide two men of Israel when the king wanted to kill them?
    Rahab hid the two men on her roof and covered them with stalks of flax.

66. What did Reuben want to do for Joseph?
    Reuben wanted to take Joseph out of the pit and send him home.

67. Why did many people leave Rehoboam and make a new king for themselves?
    Rehoboam was proud and selfish. He spoke unkindly to the people.

68. Why did Rhoda not open the gate for Peter?
    Rhoda forgot to open the gate because she was so surprised.

S.

69. How did Saul get away from the rulers while men guarded the gates?
    Some Christians let him down outside the wall in a basket.

70. Why was Shadrach living in a strange land where people worshiped idols?
    Shadrach was taken to this strange land as a captive.

71. Who did Simeon want to see before he died?
    Simeon wanted to see God's Son, the Saviour of the world.

72. What did Stephen preach that made the people so angry?
    Stephen said, "Jesus whom you killed is the Son of God."

T.

73. Did Terah worship the true God?
    No, Terah worshiped idols.

74. What did Tobiah say about the wall the Jews were building?
    Tobiah said, "The wall you are building is so weak it would fall down if a fox went up on it."

75. Who would not believe that Jesus was alive until he saw Jesus with his own eyes?

    Thomas said he would not believe that Jesus was alive until he saw Him with his own eyes.

76. Who first taught Timothy to love and obey God?

    Timothy's mother and grandmother first taught him to love and obey God.

U.

77. Who was Paul's helper?

    Paul's helper was Urbane.

78. What did Uzza do that displeased God?

    Uzza disobeyed God when he touched the ark.

79. How old was Uzziah when he was made king?

    Uzziah was sixteen years old when he was made king.

V.

80. What was Queen Vashti's punishment for not obeying the king?

    Queen Vashti could not be queen any longer.

W.

81. What will God give us if we believe in Jesus?

    If we believe in Jesus, God will give us everlasting life.

X.

82. What is the other name for King Xerxes?

    Xerxes is the Greek name for Ahasuerus.

Y.

83. What did Jesus say we should do to be His friends?

    Jesus said, "Ye are my friends, if ye do whatsoever I command you."

Z.

84. Why did Zacchaeus climb up in a tree?

    Zacchaeus climbed a tree because he wanted to see Jesus. He was a short man.

85. Who was the strange man Zipporah met at the well?

    Zipporah met Moses at the well.

86. How did David show kindness to Jonathan?

    David had Ziba bring Jonathan's son to eat at his table.

87. What happened to Zacharias because he did not believe the angel?

    Zacharias was not able to talk until his baby was born.

Bible Stories for Young Readers Series

Bible Numbers

Dictionary of Bible Animals

ABC Book of Bible People

Bible Time

Children of the Old Testament

Children of the New Testament

"Blessed is he that readeth" (Revelation 1:3).